PETER SEREFINE

A More Tyrannical King

How The Federal Government Has Become More Oppressive Than King George

Contents

Foreword

As host of The Daily Mojo radio program and podcast, and author of Spend A Little; Save A Lot Home Improvements, I understand the challenges of getting a point across to someone, teaching a group of people anything, and finding the time in which to do all of that in the first place. With that in mind, I truly admire the dedication, work, and love that Peter puts into his projects – and into this book.

Peter and I have worked "together" on the same media platform for several years, and I've realized that he has a much deeper and broader grasp of the politics and history of this great country that we all share as Americans. I've never cared for politics, but I love history – I just hated taking the tests in school! I want to hear the stories. I want to understand the WHYs of the events in the United States that have brought us to this strange point in history.

For the first time in my life, I read aloud the Declaration of Independence this year – on a live radio show. I resisted to do it in an English accent, which it begs for. I did this because I think so few people have actually taken the time to read the short document (4 pages?) and perhaps even fewer were taught its background and the WHYs of its words. To live in a country as unique as ours is and not read, much less comprehend, the document that sets up the reasons for its existence seems absurd. To understand the WHYs of our individual liberties and the responsibilities that go hand in hand with them seems like a no-brainer, but it's only in my older age that I've come to understand the importance of doing so.

While preparing for the show, I was researching some of the claims made in the Declaration, and discovered that I maybe had never known – or had simply not retained – that the infamous King George against whom the Founding Fathers were rallying the troops, may not have been the tyrannical tyrant type they'd painted him to be. There was likely some propaganda in those words written by the giants of men we know as Thomas Jefferson, Benjamin Franklin, and others. This, for some reason, had never occurred to me. It was Peter I turned to in an effort to confirm what I had been reading online, even though we all know that if it's on the interwebs, it has to be true!

Just so happened that while I was simply reigniting or reinstalling some missing data in my brain that had long been pushed aside by the day-to-day tasks of our lives – Peter was writing a book on the very subject of my questions. Life is indeed full of coincidences – or is there no such thing? My goal each day is to entertain and inform the audience of my little radio program – and Peter has been a part of the program with his weekly video Liberty Minute features. Simply saying that his lessons are valuable is an understatement at this time in history.

By putting down on video – or in this case, paper – the Who,

What, Where, When and WHYS of our nation's founding – Peter is fulfilling part of his responsibility as an American citizen to teach and defend the ways of Liberty and Justice for future generations.

I hope that you have found the passion or drive it takes to become part of the solution to America's problems. This book will no doubt fill in some of the blanks you may have in your search for the truth. Enjoy the journey, and take pride in knowing that you care enough about our kids and their kids and their kids' kids – to take the time, energy, and discipline to learn and pass along your love for Liberty, Freedom, and Justice For All.

Brad Staggs
    Radio Host/Author

Preface

In the pages that follow, we embark on a journey to explore the evolving nature of our government and its implications for our cherished principles of freedom, liberty, and limited government. This book, titled "A More Tyrannical King: How the Federal Government Has Become More Oppressive Than King George," seeks to shed light on the troubling trajectory of our nation and present a compelling case for returning to constitutional principles as the only way to preserve our republic.

From the perspective of constitutional originalism, we examine the transformation of the federal government and compare it to the era of King George III's rule. Drawing upon historical accounts, legal analyses, and philosophical insights, we delve into the various domains where the federal government has expanded its powers, encroached upon individual liberties, and assumed an alarming level of control over our lives.

Our aim is to address persuadable voters, individuals who, like us, value the ideals upon which our nation was founded and are concerned about the current state of affairs. We recognize that while people may hold diverse political beliefs, it is our shared commitment to the preservation of our republic that unites us. We seek to engage in thoughtful dialogue, presenting arguments firmly rooted in constitutional principles, empirical evidence, and historical context, in the hope of fostering a deeper understanding and inspiring renewed civic engagement.

Each chapter of this book delves into a specific aspect of our government's expansion and explores its implications for individual liberties, states' rights, and the balance of power. From the growth of the administrative state to the erosion of federalism, from the curtailing of free speech rights to the encroachments on privacy, we scrutinize the actions and policies that have led us further away from the vision of our Founding Fathers.

Throughout the chapters, we provide an abundance of facts, quotations, and statistics, all properly cited to ensure transparency and accuracy. It is our commitment to intellectual integrity and thorough research that forms the foundation of this book. By presenting a comprehensive analysis, we seek to equip readers with the knowledge and understanding necessary to evaluate the state of our government critically.

At the core of our argument is the conviction that returning to constitutional principles is the only path to save our republic. We advocate for a restoration of limited government, a reinvigoration of states' rights, and a renewed focus on individual liberties. We believe that by reclaiming the spirit of the Constitution, embracing the values of personal freedom, and empowering individuals to actively participate in civic life, we can steer our nation back towards the path envisioned by our Founding Fathers.

We recognize that our perspective as constitutional originalists may not align with every reader's viewpoint. Nevertheless, we invite you to engage in an open-minded exploration of the issues at hand. We encourage thoughtful consideration of the arguments presented, robust debate, and an examination of the evidence and historical context we offer. Our goal is not to dictate or impose our views but to stimulate critical thinking and ignite conversations that are essential for the health and future of our democracy.

As you embark on this journey through the chapters that follow, we urge you to approach the material with an open heart and an inquisitive mind. Let us together delve into the complexities of our government's expansion, confront the challenges we face, and envision a future where the principles enshrined in our Constitution are safeguarded for generations to come.

May this book serve as a catalyst for reflection, dialogue, and renewed commitment to the principles that make our republic great. Together, let us embark on a path towards reclaiming the spirit of liberty and limited government, and ensure that the flame of freedom burns bright in the hearts of every citizen.

Welcome to "A More Tyrannical King: How the Federal Government Has Become More Oppressive Than King George."

1

The Expansion of Executive Power

1.1 The Framers' Vision: A Limited Executive

1.1.1 Exploring the Founders' Intentions

The framers of the United States Constitution held a deep mistrust of concentrated power, particularly in the executive branch. Their experiences under British rule and King George's tyrannical governance shaped their vision of a limited executive. The founders sought to establish a government where power was dispersed among multiple branches, providing checks and balances to prevent any one branch from becoming too powerful.

When crafting the Constitution, the framers were keenly aware of the dangers posed by an unchecked executive. They looked to the principles of classical republicanism and the writings of Enlightenment philosophers such as John Locke and Montesquieu for guidance. Their goal was to strike a delicate balance between a government strong enough to secure the rights and liberties of the people and one restrained enough to prevent the abuse of power.

James Madison, one of the principal architects of the Constitution, expressed the need for a limited executive in Federalist No. 47:

> "The accumulation of all powers, legislative, executive, and judiciary, in the same hands, whether of one, a few, or many, and whether hereditary, self-appointed, or elective, may justly be pronounced the very definition of tyranny."

1.1.2 The Checks and Balances System

The Constitution's checks and balances system was carefully designed to ensure the diffusion of power and prevent the concentration of authority. The framers intended for Congress to be the preeminent branch, representing the will of the people and serving as a check on the executive. Additionally, the judiciary was tasked with interpreting the laws and the Constitution to ensure their alignment with the nation's founding principles.

The power of Congress lies in its ability to make laws, control the nation's purse, and provide oversight of the executive branch. Through the process of legislation, Congress is supposed to deliberate, debate, and craft laws that reflect the interests and values of the American people. This process is vital for ensuring that the executive branch remains accountable to the will of the people and operates within the bounds of the Constitution.

Alexander Hamilton, in Federalist No. 78, emphasized the importance of an independent judiciary as a check on the other branches:

> "The complete independence of the courts of justice is peculiarly essential in a limited Constitution. By a limited Constitution, I understand one which contains certain specified exceptions to the legislative authority; such, for instance, as that it shall pass no bills of attainder, no ex-post-facto laws, and the like."

The judiciary plays a crucial role in interpreting the laws and the Constitution, safeguarding individual rights, and providing a check on both the legislative and executive branches. Through judicial review, the courts can declare laws and executive actions unconstitutional, ensuring that they align with the Constitution and protecting the rights of individuals from government overreach.

1.2 The Modern Presidency: Consolidation of Power

1.2.1 The Imperial Presidency

Over time, the presidency has evolved into what some scholars refer to as the "imperial presidency." The growth of executive power has allowed presidents to wield influence and authority beyond the original intentions of the framers. This expansion has occurred through various means, including executive orders, executive agreements, and assertions of inherent executive authority.

The term "imperial presidency" was popularized by historian Arthur Schlesinger Jr. in his book of the same name. Schlesinger argued that the modern presidency had become overly powerful, with presidents exerting substantial control over domestic and foreign policy, often bypassing Congress and acting unilaterally. He contended that this consolidation of power threatened the balance envisioned by the framers and eroded the principles of democratic-republican governance.

1.2.2 Executive Orders: The Erosion of Legislative Authority

Executive orders, initially intended as directives to guide executive branch officials in implementing laws passed by Congress, have increasingly been used to bypass the legislative process altogether. Presidents, with a stroke of their pen, can now enact significant policy changes unilaterally, effectively circumventing the role of Congress in lawmaking. This erosion of legislative authority has contributed to the imbalance of power between the executive and legislative branches.

Executive orders have a long history in the United States, but their use and significance have grown substantially in recent decades. Presidents from both major political parties have employed executive orders to pursue their policy agendas when faced with congressional gridlock or as a means of expediting action on pressing issues. However, this trend undermines the constitutional role of Congress as the primary lawmaking body and circumvents the deliberative process intended by the framers.

President Barack Obama, in a 2014 interview, defended his use of executive orders:

> "We're not just going to be waiting for legislation in order to make sure that we're providing Americans the kind of help they need. I've got a pen and I've got a phone."

While presidents argue that executive orders are necessary to address urgent matters, opponents contend that their overuse undermines the separation of powers and erodes the role of Congress as the representative body of the people.

1.2.3 The Growth of the Administrative State

Another factor contributing to the consolidation of executive power is the growth of the administrative state. Executive agencies, armed with rule-making authority, have gained substantial discretion in shaping and enforcing regulations. This expansion of the administrative state has led to a proliferation of unelected bureaucrats who possess significant decision-making power, effectively sidestepping the constitutional principle of separation of powers.

The administrative state refers to the vast network of federal agencies and departments responsible for implementing and enforcing laws passed by Congress. Over time, these agencies have assumed greater authority, often crafting regulations that have the force of law without direct congressional approval. This growth has been driven by various factors, including the complexity of modern governance, technological advancements, and the delegation of legislative power by Congress to administrative agencies.

Ronald Reagan, in his 1981 inaugural address, highlighted the dangers of an unchecked administrative state:

"It is no coincidence that our present troubles parallel and are proportionate to the intervention and intrusion in our lives that result from unnecessary and excessive growth of government."

Critics argue that the expansion of the administrative state undermines accountability, as unelected bureaucrats wield significant power over the lives of citizens without the same level of scrutiny and accountability as elected officials.

1.3 A Comparison: King George vs. the Modern Executive

1.3.1 Executive Overreach: Then and Now

While King George's abuses of power are well-documented in American history, it is essential to recognize the parallels between his tyrannical rule and the modern executive's overreach. Both instances involve the concentration of power in a single individual or institution, resulting in a diminishing role for the people and their elected representatives.

During the American Revolution, the colonists experienced firsthand the consequences of an executive who wielded unchecked power. King George III asserted authority over the colonies, disregarding their rights and imposing burdensome taxes without their consent. The grievances listed in the Declaration of Independence, including

> "He has combined with others to subject us to a jurisdiction foreign to our Constitution and unacknowledged by our laws" and "He has erected a multitude of new offices, and sent hither swarms of officers to harass our people and eat out their substance,"

reflect the abuses suffered under King George's rule.

Thomas Jefferson, in a letter to John Taylor in 1816, cautioned against the dangers of executive overreach:

> "The concentrating these in the same hands is precisely the definition of Despotic government. It will be no alleviation that these powers will be exercised by a plurality of hands: all three branches of them will be in the same hands."

Jefferson's words resonate with the concerns regarding the concentration of power in the modern executive, as multiple branches of government are increasingly controlled or influenced by the executive branch.

1.3.2 Executive Power and Individual Liberty

The expansion of executive power poses a direct threat to individual liberty. As the executive branch amasses more authority, the ability of citizens to participate in the political process and influence policy diminishes. Moreover, an over-reaching executive can infringe upon constitutional rights, such as freedom of speech, due process, and privacy. It is crucial to restore the balance of power and rein in the executive to protect the rights and liberties of the American people.

President Abraham Lincoln, in his 1861 inaugural address, emphasized the importance of preserving individual liberties even during times of crisis:

> "Our reliance is in the love of liberty which God has planted in our bosoms. Our defense is in the preservation of the spirit which prizes liberty as the heritage of all men, in all lands, everywhere."

Lincoln recognized that safeguarding individual liberties is a cornerstone of a just and free society, and any encroachment upon these liberties must be resisted.

In the comparison between King George's rule and the modern executive's overreach, there are striking similarities. Both instances involve the concentration of power in a single individual or institution, resulting in a diminishing role for the people and their elected representatives. The abuses suffered under

King George's tyranny, such as taxation without representation, denial of basic rights, and a lack of recourse for grievances, find echoes in the modern executive's expansion of power beyond constitutional limits.

To protect the principles of individual liberty, representative governance, and the rule of law, it is imperative to restore the balance of power and ensure that the executive branch operates within the bounds set forth by the Constitution. The framers' vision of a limited executive, where power is dispersed and checked by the other branches, remains crucial in safeguarding the rights and liberties of the American people.

Conclusion:

In examining the framers' vision of a limited executive, the consolidation of power in the modern presidency, and the comparison between King George's rule and the modern executive's overreach, it becomes evident that the federal government has strayed far from its constitutional roots. The expansion of executive power undermines the principles of checks and balances, erodes the authority of Congress, and poses a threat to individual liberty.

The framers' wisdom and foresight in crafting a system of government that limits executive power and ensures the participation and representation of the people cannot be understated. To save our republic and preserve the rights and liberties enshrined in the Constitution, we must recognize the dangers of an unchecked executive and advocate for a return to the constitutional principles that once ensured the protection of our fundamental rights.

References:

- Madison, James. "The Federalist No. 47 - The Particular Structure of the New Government and the Distribution of Power among Its Different Parts." 1788.
- Hamilton, Alexander. "The Federalist No. 78 - The Judiciary Department." 1788.
- Schlesinger Jr., Arthur M. "The Imperial Presidency." 1973.
- Obama, Barack. Interview with YouTube Creators. January 22, 2014.
- Reagan, Ronald. Inaugural Address. January 20, 1981.
- Jefferson, Thomas. Letter to John Taylor. May 28, 1816.
- Lincoln, Abraham. First Inaugural Address. March 4, 1861.

2

The Supremacy of the Federal Government

2.1 Federalism and Limited Government

2.1.1 The Founders' Vision of Federalism

The framers of the United States Constitution recognized the importance of federalism in maintaining a balance of power between the federal government and the states. They envisioned a system where the federal government had limited, enumerated powers, while the states retained substantial authority to govern within their respective jurisdictions. This division of powers was intended to prevent the concentration of authority in a centralized government and to protect individual liberties.

Alexander Hamilton, in Federalist No. 17, explained the benefits of federalism:

> "The fabric of American empire ought to rest on the solid basis of THE CONSENT OF THE PEOPLE. The streams of national power ought to flow immediately from that pure, original fountain of all legitimate authority."

Hamilton emphasized that the power of the federal government derived from the consent of the people, and the states played a vital role in ensuring this consent was preserved.

2.1.2 The Tenth Amendment: Reserving Powers to the States

The Tenth Amendment to the United States Constitution further reinforces the principles of federalism by reserving powers not delegated to the federal government to the states or the people. It serves as a safeguard against the encroachment of federal authority on matters that should be within the purview of state governments. The Tenth Amendment acts as a reminder that the federal government's powers are limited and that the states possess inherent sovereignty.

James Madison, in a speech before the House of Representatives in 1789, emphasized the importance of the Tenth Amendment:

"The powers delegated by the proposed Constitution to the federal government are few and defined. Those which are to remain in the State governments are numerous and indefinite. The former will be exercised principally on external objects, as war, peace, negotiation, and foreign commerce. The powers reserved to the several States will extend to all the objects which, in the ordinary course of affairs, concern the lives, liberties, and properties of the people, and the internal order, improvement, and prosperity of the State."

2.2 The Federal Leviathan

2.2.1 Expansion of the Commerce Clause

One area where the federal government's power has expanded significantly is through the interpretation of the Commerce Clause of the Constitution. Originally intended to regulate interstate commerce and prevent trade barriers between the states, the Commerce Clause has been broadly interpreted, granting the federal government authority over a wide range of activities that were once considered within the realm of state authority.

The landmark Supreme Court case of Gibbons v. Ogden

(1824) established a broad interpretation of the Commerce Clause, asserting that the federal government had the power to regulate not only the physical movement of goods but also economic activities that have a substantial effect on interstate commerce. This expansive interpretation has allowed the federal government to intervene in areas such as labor relations, environmental regulation, and healthcare, exerting significant influence over the states and eroding their sovereignty.

Another significant instance showcasing the broadening interpretation of the commerce clause emerged in the case of Wickard v. Filburn, 317 U.S. 111 (1942). The case revolved around Roscoe Filburn, a small-scale Ohio farmer who exceeded his allotted wheat production by nearly 12 acres under federal regulation. Filburn consumed the excess wheat on his own farm and did not engage in any sales, whether interstate or intrastate. However, the Supreme Court ruled that Filburn's non-participation in commerce still had an impact on commerce, leading to a violation of the regulation. This case underscores the expansive scope given to the commerce clause and its implications for federal regulatory authority.

2.2.2 Unfunded Mandates and Coercive Federalism

Another manifestation of federal government overreach is the imposition of unfunded mandates on the states. Unfunded mandates refer to federal requirements placed on state and local governments without providing adequate funding to implement them. This practice places a financial burden on the states and undermines their ability to allocate resources effectively and address the needs of their citizens.

Coercive federalism, characterized by the federal government using its financial leverage to compel states to adopt specific policies or programs, further erodes state sovereignty. Through conditional grants and funding incentives, the federal government can influence state policies and actions, effectively coercing compliance with federal directives. This undermines the principles of federalism and diminishes the ability of states to govern according to their unique circumstances and the preferences of their citizens.

2.3 A Comparison: King George vs. Federal Overreach

2.3.1 Centralized Authority: Then and Now

The centralization of authority witnessed under King George III's rule bears resemblance to the encroachment of federal power on state sovereignty. Just as King George sought to exert control over the American colonies from afar, the federal government has expanded its authority beyond its enumerated powers, infringing on matters traditionally left to the states. Both instances demonstrate the danger of centralized authority and its potential to undermine the principles of federalism and limit the autonomy of local governance.

2.3.2 States' Rights and Individual Liberties

State governments, as laboratories of democracy, have historically played a vital role in protecting individual liberties and ensuring diverse policy approaches that reflect the values and preferences of their citizens. The erosion of state sovereignty and the expansion of federal power threaten this important role. As federal authority expands, the ability of states to address the specific needs and desires of their populations is diminished, potentially infringing upon the rights and freedoms of individuals.

The founders recognized the importance of states' rights as a bulwark against tyranny. Thomas Jefferson, in a letter to William H. Crawford in 1816, stated:

> "Our country is too large to have all its affairs directed by a single government. Public servants at such a distance, and from under the eye of their constituents, must, from the circumstance of distance, be unable to administer and overlook all the details necessary for the good government of the citizens, and the same circumstance, by rendering detection impossible to their constituents, will invite the public agents to corruption, plunder, and waste."

Conclusion:

The principles of federalism and the reservation of powers to the states play a crucial role in safeguarding the balance of power and protecting individual liberties. The framers of the Constitution intended for the federal government to have limited, enumerated powers, with the states retaining significant authority to govern within their jurisdictions. However, the expansion of the federal government's authority, particularly through expansive interpretations of the Commerce Clause, unfunded mandates, and coercive federalism, has undermined the principles of federalism and eroded state sovereignty.

To preserve the integrity of our federal system and protect the rights and liberties of the American people, it is essential to restore a proper balance between the federal government and the states. Recognizing the value of states as laboratories of democracy and allowing them the autonomy to address the unique needs and preferences of their citizens is paramount. By embracing the principles of federalism, we can ensure that government remains responsive, accountable, and closer to the people it serves.

References:

- Hamilton, Alexander. "The Federalist No. 17 - The Same Subject Continued: The Insufficiency of the Present Confederation to Preserve the Union." 1787.

- Madison, James. "The Federalist No. 45 - The Alleged Danger from the Powers of the Union to the State Governments Considered." 1788.
- Wickard v. Filburn, 317 U.S. 111 (1942)
- Madison, James. Speech before the House of Representatives. June 8, 1789.
- Jefferson, Thomas. Letter to William H. Crawford. March 15, 1816.
- Gibbons v. Ogden, 22 U.S. 1 (1824).

3

The Erosion of Individual Rights

3.1 The Bill of Rights: Safeguarding Individual Liberties

3.1.1 The Importance of Individual Rights

The framers of the United States Constitution recognized the fundamental importance of protecting individual rights from government infringement. They sought to create a system of government that would secure the natural rights of the people and prevent the abuses they had experienced under British rule. As a result, the Bill of Rights, comprising the first ten amendments to the Constitution, was adopted to specifically enumerate and protect individual liberties.

James Madison, in a speech before the House of Representatives in 1789, highlighted the significance of individual rights:

"It is a fundamental principle that the powers of a government are derived from the consent of the governed. The Bill of Rights... announce[s] great principles, securing to the people their civil and political rights."

3.1.2 The First Amendment: Freedom of Speech and Religion

The First Amendment of the United States Constitution guarantees the freedom of speech and religion, two fundamental rights that are central to a free society. Freedom of speech allows individuals to express their opinions, engage in public discourse, and challenge the status quo without fear of government reprisal. Freedom of religion ensures that individuals can worship according to their beliefs or practice no religion at all, free from government interference.

Thomas Jefferson, in a letter to the Danbury Baptist Association in 1802, famously expressed the principle of separation between church and state:

"Believing with you that religion is a matter which lies solely between Man & his God, that he owes account to none other for his faith or his worship, that the legitimate powers of government reach actions only, & not opinions, I contemplate with sovereign reverence that act of the whole American people which declared that their legislature should 'make no law respecting an establishment of religion, or prohibiting the free exercise thereof,' thus building a wall of separation between Church & State."

3.1.3 The Second Amendment: The Right to Bear Arms

The Second Amendment of the Constitution guarantees the right of the people to keep and bear arms. It recognizes the individual's right to self-defense and the importance of an armed citizenry as a safeguard against tyranny. The right to bear arms has been a subject of ongoing debate, with varying interpretations of its scope and limitations.

Thomas Jefferson, in a letter to William Smith in 1787, emphasized the significance of an armed citizenry:

"What country can preserve its liberties if its rulers are not warned from time to time that their people preserve the spirit of resistance? Let them take arms."

3.2 The Erosion of Civil Liberties

3.2.1 National Security and the Fourth Amendment

In the name of national security, the federal government has increasingly encroached upon the Fourth Amendment protections against unreasonable searches and seizures. Surveillance programs, such as the warrantless collection of phone metadata, have raised concerns about privacy and the scope of government surveillance powers. The expansion of surveillance technologies and practices threatens the right to privacy that is essential for a free society.

Benjamin Franklin, in a letter to Charles Humphreys in 1789, eloquently stated:

> "Those who would give up essential Liberty, to purchase a little temporary Safety, deserve neither Liberty nor Safety."

3.2.2 Due Process and the Fifth and Sixth Amendments

The Fifth and Sixth Amendments of the Constitution safeguard due process rights, ensuring fair treatment, and protecting individuals accused of crimes. These amendments guarantee the right to a fair and speedy trial, the right to confront witnesses, and the right against self-incrimination.

John Adams, a key figure in the American Revolution and the second President of the United States, emphasized the importance of due process:

> "It is more important that innocence should be protected than it is that guilt should be punished."

3.2.3 Emerging Challenges: Technology and Individual Rights

Advancements in technology have brought about new challenges to individual rights. Issues such as digital privacy, government access to electronic communications, and the use of facial recognition technology raise concerns about the protection of individual liberties in the digital age. Balancing the need for security with the preservation of civil liberties remains an ongoing challenge for the modern society.

Justice Louis Brandeis, in his dissenting opinion in Olmstead v. United States (1928), recognized the potential threats posed by technological advancements:

"~~The~~ progress of science in furnishing the government with means of espionage is not likely to stop with wiretapping. Ways may someday be developed by which the government, without removing papers from secret drawers, can reproduce them in court, and by which it will be enabled to expose to a jury the most intimate occurrences of the home."

3.3 A Comparison: King George vs. Modern Intrusions

3.3.1 Surveillance and Unreasonable Searches

The invasive surveillance practices and unreasonable searches conducted by the British authorities during colonial times bear similarities to modern encroachments on civil liberties. Just as the colonists objected to unwarranted searches of their homes and belongings, contemporary concerns arise over government surveillance programs that collect vast amounts of personal data without proper oversight or reasonable suspicion.

3.3.2 Balancing Security and Civil Liberties

The tension between security and civil liberties persists throughout history. King George's claims of needing to maintain order and security to justify infringements on colonial rights find echoes in contemporary debates surrounding national security measures and the erosion of individual liberties. Striking a balance between safeguarding public safety and upholding civil liberties remains a challenge that requires constant vigilance and adherence to constitutional principles.

Conclusion:

The erosion of individual rights and civil liberties threatens the very essence of a free society. The framers of the Constitution recognized the importance of protecting these rights and enshrined them in the Bill of Rights. However, the encroachments on free speech, religious freedom, privacy, and due process demonstrate the need for continued vigilance and defense of these fundamental liberties.

As technology advances and new challenges emerge, it is vital to ensure that individual rights are not sacrificed in the name of security or expediency. The wisdom of the framers and the voices of those who have championed individual liberties throughout history serve as a reminder that the preservation of civil liberties is essential for a just and free society.

References:

- Madison, James. Speech before the House of Representatives. June 8, 1789.
- Jefferson, Thomas. Letter to the Danbury Baptist Association. January 1, 1802.
- Jefferson, Thomas. Letter to William Smith. November 13, 1787.
- Franklin, Benjamin. Letter to Charles Humphreys. November 11, 1789.
- Adams, John. Defense of the Constitutions. 1787.
- Brandeis, Louis. Olmstead v. United States, 277 U.S. 438 (1928).

4

Judicial Activism and the Erosion of Constitutional Interpretation

4.1 The Role of the Judiciary: Guardians of the Constitution

4.1.1 Judicial Review: Safeguarding Constitutional Rights

The judiciary serves as a critical branch of government responsible for interpreting and applying the Constitution. At the heart of the judiciary's role lies the power of judicial review, the authority to review laws, executive actions, and government policies to ensure their constitutionality. Judicial review acts as a vital safeguard, protecting individual rights and preserving the integrity of the Constitution.

> "The interpretation of the laws is the proper and peculiar province of the courts. A constitution is, in fact, and must be regarded by the judges, as a fundamental law. It, therefore, belongs to them to ascertain its meaning as well as the meaning of any particular act proceeding from the legislative body." - Alexander Hamilton, The Federalist No. 78

The concept of judicial review was established in the landmark Supreme Court case Marbury v. Madison (1803). Chief Justice John Marshall asserted that it was the duty of the courts to interpret the Constitution and determine whether laws aligned with its provisions. This power, he argued, was inherent in the judiciary's responsibility to uphold the rule of law and ensure the supremacy of the Constitution.

4.1.2 Constitutional Interpretation: Originalism and Living Constitution

Constitutional interpretation approaches can be broadly categorized into two main schools of thought: originalism and the living Constitution theory. Originalism emphasizes interpreting the Constitution according to its original public meaning at the time of its adoption. This approach seeks to anchor constitutional interpretation in the text, structure, and historical context of the Constitution.

Supporters of originalism argue that it provides a reliable and consistent method of interpreting the Constitution, as it ties constitutional principles to the intentions of the framers and the understanding of the ratifying public. By adhering to the original meaning, originalists contend that judges can avoid imposing their own policy preferences and respect the representative process.

> "Originalism is not a modern invention… It is old and proven… It is the only approach to constitutional interpretation that has any prospect of establishing a judiciary that respects the Constitution." - Justice Antonin Scalia

In contrast, the living Constitution theory posits that the Constitution is a dynamic document that must evolve to meet the changing needs and values of society. Advocates of the living Constitution theory argue that the framers intentionally left the Constitution's language broad and flexible to accommodate future generations' interpretations and advancements in societal understanding.

4.2 Judicial Activism: Exceeding Constitutional Bounds

4.2.1 Defining Judicial Activism

Judicial activism refers to a judicial approach where judges go beyond interpreting the law and instead shape or create policy through their decisions. Activist judges may engage in judicial policymaking, redefining legal concepts or inventing new rights that are not explicitly mentioned or intended by the framers of the Constitution. This practice raises concerns about the proper role of the judiciary in a free society.

> "The temptation to grasp and wield the powers of government is not absent from the judiciary. It must be resisted. It is essential to maintaining the legitimacy of judicial authority in our democratic society." - Justice Sandra Day O'Connor

Judicial activism undermines the separation of powers, encroaches upon the authority of the legislative and executive branches, and disrupts the representative process. Instead of adhering to the text and original meaning of the Constitution, activist judges may seek to impose their own policy preferences, potentially substituting their judgment for that of the elected representatives of the people.

4.2.2 Overstepping Constitutional Boundaries

One of the primary criticisms of judicial activism is that it enables judges to overstep their constitutional boundaries, effectively legislating from the bench. By creating new rights or expanding existing ones beyond their original scope, activist judges may reshape society and override the will of the people as expressed through their elected representatives.

> "The liberties of our country, the freedom of our civil constitution, are worth defending against all hazards."
> - Samuel Adams

The implications of judicial activism can extend beyond individual cases, as it sets legal precedents that influence future decisions and potentially alter the interpretation of the Constitution itself. Critics argue that this approach diminishes the role of the legislature, circumvents the established process, and undermines the principle of limited government envisioned by the framers.

4.3 The Impact of Judicial Activism

4.3.1 Uncertainty and Instability in the Law

One consequence of judicial activism is the introduction of uncertainty and instability in the legal system. When judges engage in policy making, their decisions may lack clear grounding in the Constitution's text, historical context, or original intent. This uncertainty can make it challenging for individuals and institutions to navigate the law and anticipate how it will be applied in different contexts.

> "Guard with jealous attention the public liberty. Suspect everyone who approaches that jewel. Unfortunately, nothing will preserve it but downright force. Whenever you give up that force, you are inevitably ruined." - Patrick Henry

The unpredictability resulting from judicial activism raises concerns about the rule of law, as legal principles may shift based on the personal preferences and ideological inclinations of judges. This departure from a stable and consistent legal framework undermines public confidence in the judiciary and hampers the effective functioning of the legal system.

4.3.2 Public Accountability and Representative Governance

The principle of representative governance relies on elected representatives making policy decisions in response to the will of the people. Judicial activism, by circumventing the representative process, reduces public accountability and places decision-making power in the hands of unelected judges. This shift of power from elected representatives to the judiciary can undermine the legitimacy of policy outcomes and impede the ability of citizens to influence the laws that govern them.

Judges, as appointed officials with life tenure, should exercise judicial restraint and defer to the legislative and executive branches whenever possible. This deference allows elected officials to shape policy in accordance with the evolving needs and preferences of the citizenry, rather than imposing top-down decisions that may not reflect the will of the people.

4.4 A Comparison: King George vs. Judicial Overreach

4.4.1 Concentration of Power: Historical Parallels

The concentration of power witnessed under King George III's rule during the colonial period shares similarities with judicial overreach. Both instances involve the unchecked exercise of authority that undermines the principles of limited government and threatens individual liberties. Just as the colonists resisted King George's encroachments on their rights, contemporary concerns arise when judges exceed their constitutional bounds and impose their policy preferences.

4.4.2 Restoring Judicial Restraint and Constitutional Balance

To preserve the integrity of the judiciary and uphold the principles of republican governance, it is essential to restore judicial restraint. Judicial restraint requires judges to adhere to the text and original meaning of the Constitution, respect the representative process, and defer to the elected branches of government when interpreting statutes or making policy decisions.

By embracing judicial restraint, judges can strike a balance between protecting individual rights and respecting the will of the people. Upholding the separation of powers and adhering to the principles of limited government are crucial for maintaining the judiciary's integrity and ensuring that constitutional interpretation remains faithful to the framers' vision.

Conclusion:

The judiciary's role as the guardian of the Constitution is essential in upholding individual rights, preserving the rule of law, and maintaining the delicate balance of power among the branches of government. While judicial activism threatens the proper functioning of our republican system, a commitment to constitutional interpretation grounded in originalism and judicial restraint can safeguard the integrity of the judiciary and the principles enshrined in the Constitution.

By adhering to the text, structure, and historical context of the Constitution, judges can ensure that their decisions are rooted in the representative process and the original intentions of the framers. Striking the right balance between judicial independence and respect for the separation of powers is crucial for preserving the rule of law, accountability, and the enduring principles upon which our republic was founded.

References:

- Marshall, John. Marbury v. Madison, 5 U.S. (1 Cranch) 137 (1803).
- Scalia, Antonin. "Originalism: The Lesser Evil." University of Cincinnati Law Review 57, no. 4 (1989): 849-66.
- O'Connor, Sandra Day. "The Challenges Facing the Judiciary." Cardozo Law Review 14, no. 3 (1992): 771-78.

5

The Administrative State: Unchecked Bureaucratic Power

5.1 The Rise of the Administrative State

5.1.1 The Expansion of the Executive Branch

Over time, the executive branch of the federal government has expanded, giving rise to what is commonly known as the administrative state. The administrative state encompasses a vast network of bureaucratic agencies and departments that exercise significant regulatory authority. This growth of administrative power has raised concerns about the concentration of power and the potential for unchecked bureaucratic influence.

The expansion of the administrative state can be traced back to the Progressive Era in the early 20th century when there was a push for more government involvement in economic and social affairs. As the federal government assumed greater responsibility for regulating various aspects of society, administrative agencies were created to implement and enforce these regulations.

> "If Congress can do whatever in their discretion can be done by money, and will promote the general welfare, the government is no longer a limited one, possessing enumerated powers, but an indefinite one." - James Madison

5.1.2 Delegation of Legislative Power

One key characteristic of the administrative state is the delegation of legislative power from Congress to administrative agencies. Congress often passes broad and ambiguous laws, leaving the details and implementation to administrative agencies. This delegation allows agencies to create regulations and make policy decisions that have significant effects on businesses, individuals, and society as a whole.

The delegation of legislative power raises concerns about the separation of powers and the accountability of these agencies. As unelected bureaucrats gain the authority to shape and enforce regulations, questions arise about their accountability to the people and the potential for regulatory overreach.

5.2 Regulatory Overreach and the Erosion of Accountability

5.2.1 Rule-making and Regulatory Impact

Administrative agencies possess the power to issue rules and regulations that have the force of law. These regulations can significantly impact businesses, individuals, and the economy. While regulations are intended to protect the public interest and promote safety and welfare, concerns arise when agencies exceed their authority or create burdensome and unnecessary regulations.

> "The government of the United States is a definite government, confined to specified objects. It is not like state governments, whose powers are more general. Charity is no part of the legislative duty of the government." - James Madison

The sheer volume and complexity of regulations make it difficult for businesses and individuals to navigate the regulatory landscape. Compliance costs can be substantial, especially for small businesses, stifling innovation and economic growth. The regulatory burden can also impede individual liberties by imposing restrictions on personal choices and limiting the flexibility of individuals to make decisions that best suit their circumstances.

5.2.2 Lack of Accountability

One of the key challenges posed by the administrative state is the lack of direct democratic accountability. Unlike elected representatives, who can be held accountable by the voters, administrative agencies are staffed by unelected bureaucrats. These bureaucrats, while tasked with implementing and enforcing regulations, are not directly accountable to the people.

The absence of democratic accountability raises concerns about the responsiveness and transparency of administrative decision-making. When agencies possess significant regulatory power without effective checks and balances, it can lead to a democratic deficit, as the public's ability to influence and shape regulations becomes limited.

5.3 Restoring Accountability and Constitutional Balance

5.3.1 Congressional Oversight and Reining in the Administrative State

To address the concerns associated with the administrative state, it is essential to restore accountability and proper constitutional balance. One way to achieve this is through robust congressional oversight. Congress has the responsibility to monitor and hold administrative agencies accountable for their actions. By conducting rigorous oversight hearings, demanding transparency, and reviewing agency regulations, Congress can ensure that administrative agencies operate within their delegated authority and serve the public interest.

> "We must return to the principles and values that guided our Founding Fathers. The Constitution provides the blueprint for a limited government that respects individual liberties and ensures a system of checks and balances." - Mike Lee

Additionally, Congress has the power to reform and streamline the regulatory process. By crafting clearer and more precise laws, Congress can minimize the need for extensive agency rule-making and provide greater guidance to administrative agencies. This approach helps maintain the separation of powers and ensures that policy decisions are made by elected representatives who are accountable to the people.

5.3.2 Judicial Review of Administrative Actions

Another essential safeguard against regulatory overreach is the judiciary's role in reviewing administrative actions. Courts can assess whether administrative agencies have exceeded their statutory authority or violated constitutional limits. Judicial review ensures that agency decisions are consistent with the law and do not infringe upon individual rights or encroach upon the authority of other branches of government.

To enhance the effectiveness of judicial review, it is crucial for courts to adhere to the principles of originalism and statutory interpretation. By applying a rigorous and faithful interpretation of the law, courts can provide a check on administrative agencies, preventing them from exceeding their authority and protecting individual liberties.

5.4 A Comparison: King George vs. Unchecked Bureaucratic Power

5.4.1 Concentration of Power: Historical Parallels

The concentration of power witnessed under King George III's rule and the growth of the administrative state share similarities. Both instances involve the centralization of authority and the potential for abuses of power. Just as the colonists resisted King George's overreach, concerns arise when administrative agencies exert regulatory control without proper accountability or effective checks on their authority.

5.4.2 Restoring Constitutional Balance

To restore constitutional balance and ensure that the administrative state operates within its proper limits, it is essential to address the concerns associated with regulatory overreach and lack of democratic accountability. Robust congressional oversight, clear legislative guidance, and effective judicial review are crucial components of restoring accountability and protecting individual liberties.

> "The separation of powers and the system of checks and balances are essential safeguards against the concentration of power. We must strengthen these principles to protect the integrity of our democratic institutions." - Ted Cruz

By promoting transparency, reducing regulatory burdens, and ensuring that administrative agencies act within the boundaries set by the Constitution and the law, we can strike a balance that preserves the republican principles upon which our nation was founded.

Conclusion:

The growth of the administrative state and the concentration of power in bureaucratic agencies raise concerns about democratic accountability, regulatory overreach, and the erosion of constitutional principles. Restoring accountability, proper checks and balances, and constitutional balance are necessary to address these concerns.

Through robust congressional oversight, clear legislative guidance, and rigorous judicial review, we can ensure that administrative agencies operate within their delegated authority, respect individual liberties, and remain accountable to the people. By safeguarding the principles of republican governance and upholding the Constitution, we can strike a balance that allows for effective governance while preserving the rights and liberties of the American people.

References:

- Lovett, Laura E. "The Administrative State and Its Discontents: Judicial Restraint and the Limits of Executive Power." Cornell Law Review 102, no. 4 (2017): 809-55.
- Mashaw, Jerry L. Creating the Administrative Constitution: The Lost One Hundred Years of American Administrative Law. New Haven: Yale University Press, 2012.
- Sunstein, Cass R. "Beyond Marbury: The Executive's Power to Say What the Law Is." Yale Law Journal 115, no. 2 (2005): 258-458.

6

Economic Liberty and the Threat of Government Overregulation

6.1 The Importance of Economic Liberty

6.1.1 The Foundations of Economic Freedom

Economic liberty, the freedom to engage in voluntary economic activities, is a fundamental aspect of individual liberty and a cornerstone of a prosperous society. The framers of the Constitution recognized the significance of economic freedom and sought to create a system that protected property rights, encouraged entrepreneurship, and fostered free markets.

> "The free market is the greatest generator of wealth in the history of the world. It has lifted billions of people out of poverty and has led to unprecedented

innovation and prosperity." - Paul Ryan

The framers understood that economic freedom was essential for individuals to pursue their own economic interests, engage in productive activities, and contribute to the overall prosperity of the nation. By enshrining the protection of property rights in the Constitution, they aimed to create an environment where individuals could enjoy the fruits of their labor, invest in new ventures, and reap the rewards of their economic endeavors.

6.1.2 The Benefits of Free Markets

Free markets, characterized by voluntary exchanges and minimal government intervention, have been instrumental in driving economic growth, innovation, and prosperity. In a free market system, individuals are free to engage in economic activities based on their own choices, preferences, and abilities. This economic freedom allows for the efficient allocation of resources, the creation of wealth, and the satisfaction of consumers' needs and desires.

The operation of free markets is driven by the principles of supply and demand, competition, and the pursuit of self-interest. Through competition, businesses strive to offer better products, services, and prices, resulting in increased efficiency and improved consumer welfare. Free markets incentivize innovation, encourage entrepreneurship, and foster economic mobility, allowing individuals to improve their economic well-being and pursue their aspirations.

6.2 The Threat of Government Overregulation

6.2.1 Regulatory Burdens on Businesses

While regulations are necessary to protect public health, safety, and the environment, excessive government regulations can stifle economic growth, innovation, and individual freedom. Overregulation imposes significant burdens on businesses, particularly small and medium-sized enterprises, inhibiting their ability to compete, create jobs, and contribute to economic prosperity.

> "Economic growth and the protection of individual liberty are inextricably linked. Excessive government intervention stifles innovation, discourages entrepreneurship, and undermines economic freedom."
> - Rand Paul

The cumulative impact of numerous and often overlapping regulations can lead to increased compliance costs, reduced investment, and diminished entrepreneurial activity. Small businesses, in particular, face significant challenges in navigating the complex web of regulations, which can divert resources away from productive activities and hinder their growth and sustainability.

6.2.2 Regulatory Capture and Cronyism

Government overregulation can create an environment ripe for regulatory capture and cronyism, where powerful special interests influence regulations to serve their own economic or political interests. When regulations become tools for rent-seeking and favoritism, the competitive dynamics of free markets are distorted, and the interests of the few supersede those of the many.

Regulatory capture occurs when regulatory agencies are captured by the industries they are meant to oversee, leading to regulations that benefit specific companies or interest groups at the expense of competition and the general public. This form of capture undermines the level playing field, stifles innovation, and hampers economic mobility. It erodes public trust in the fairness and impartiality of the regulatory process, exacerbating concerns about the concentration of economic power and the erosion of economic liberty.

6.3 Restoring Economic Freedom

6.3.1 Regulatory Reform and Streamlining

To protect and restore economic freedom, it is crucial to engage in comprehensive regulatory reform and streamline the regulatory process. Government agencies should undertake systematic reviews of existing regulations to identify and eliminate unnecessary, outdated, or overly burdensome rules. By promoting regulatory efficiency and effectiveness, we can strike a balance that safeguards public interests while minimizing the burdens on businesses and individuals.

Furthermore, it is essential to improve transparency and public participation in the rule-making process. Public input and feedback can help ensure that regulations are crafted with careful consideration of their impact on economic liberty, individual rights, and the overall well-being of society. Implementing mechanisms such as regulatory impact assessments, cost-benefit analyses, and sunset provisions can enhance accountability and prevent the accumulation of unnecessary regulations.

6.3.2 Promoting Competition and Level Playing Field

To foster economic liberty, it is imperative to promote competition and maintain a level playing field in the marketplace. Antitrust enforcement plays a crucial role in preventing the concentration of economic power and ensuring that markets remain competitive. Vigilance against monopolistic practices, anti-competitive behavior, and unfair market practices helps protect consumer choice, encourage innovation, and support economic freedom.

In addition to antitrust measures, efforts should be made to reduce barriers to entry and promote entrepreneurship.

Policies that encourage access to capital, provide support for small businesses, simplify licensing requirements, and promote innovation and technological advancement can unleash the entrepreneurial spirit and facilitate economic mobility. Nurturing a business-friendly environment and supporting economic diversification can create opportunities for individuals to pursue their economic aspirations and contribute to the overall prosperity of society.

6.4 A Comparison: King George vs. Economic Liberty

6.4.1 Economic Constraints and Colonial Resistance

The economic constraints imposed by King George's government on the American colonies sparked resistance and played a significant role in the fight for independence. The colonists objected to excessive taxation, trade restrictions, and monopolistic practices that hindered economic freedom, stifled their ability to pursue economic opportunities, and impeded their economic well-being.

The struggle for economic liberty during colonial times highlighted the importance of protecting individual economic rights, preserving property rights, and maintaining a favorable environment for economic growth and innovation.

6.4.2 Preserving Economic Liberty Today

Preserving economic liberty requires a commitment to limiting government intervention, reducing regulatory burdens, and fostering an environment that encourages free markets and entrepreneurial activities. Just as the colonists resisted economic constraints imposed by King George's government, it is essential for us to advocate for limited government and promote policies that protect and enhance economic freedom. By upholding the principles of economic liberty, we can ensure that individuals have the opportunity to pursue their economic aspirations and enjoy the benefits of a thriving and dynamic economy.

Preserving economic liberty requires a multifaceted approach that encompasses not only regulatory reform but also education and public awareness. It is crucial to educate individuals about the value of economic freedom, the benefits of free markets, and the potential dangers of excessive government intervention. By fostering a greater understanding of economic principles and their real-world implications, we can build a society that values and protects economic liberty as an essential component of individual freedom and overall societal well-being.

Conclusion:

Economic liberty, grounded in free markets, property rights, and limited government intervention, is fundamental to individual freedom, economic growth, and societal prosperity. Excessive government overregulation poses a significant threat to economic freedom by impeding innovation, hindering entrepreneurship, and distorting market dynamics.

To preserve economic liberty, we must engage in comprehensive regulatory reform, streamline the regulatory process, and promote transparency and public participation. By fostering competition, preventing regulatory capture, and reducing barriers to entry, we can create an environment that encourages entrepreneurship, innovation, and economic mobility.

As we reflect on the struggles for economic liberty during the colonial era, we recognize the enduring importance of protecting individual economic rights and fostering an environment conducive to economic growth and prosperity. By upholding the principles of economic freedom, we can build a society that thrives on individual initiative, innovation, and the pursuit of economic well-being for the benefit of all.

References:

- Madison, James. The Federalist No. 10. 1787.
- Friedman, Milton. Capitalism and Freedom. University of Chicago Press, 1962.
- Baumol, William J., Litan, Robert E., and Schramm, Carl J. Good Capitalism, Bad Capitalism, and the Economics of Growth and Prosperity. Yale University Press, 2007.
- Hazlett, Thomas W. The Political Spectrum: The Tumul-

tuous Liberation of Wireless Technology, from Herbert Hoover to the Smartphone. Yale University Press, 2017.

- Stigler, George J. The Theory of Economic Regulation. The Bell Journal of Economics and Management Science, 1971.

7

Free Speech and the Threat of Censorship

7.1 The Importance of Free Speech

7.1.1 Free Speech as a Pillar of Freedom

Free speech is a fundamental pillar of free societies, serving as the cornerstone of open discourse, public debate, and the exchange of ideas. The framers of the Constitution recognized the paramount importance of free speech in safeguarding individual liberties and ensuring a robust marketplace of ideas.

The First Amendment to the United States Constitution explicitly protects the freedom of speech, recognizing its critical role in the functioning of a free society. Free speech allows citizens to express their opinions, challenge prevailing beliefs, engage in political discourse, and hold those in power accountable.

7.1.2 Promoting Intellectual Diversity

A vibrant and diverse marketplace of ideas fosters intellectual growth, innovation, and societal progress. By protecting free speech, we create an environment where different perspectives can be heard, allowing for a more comprehensive understanding of complex issues.

Intellectual diversity encourages critical thinking, challenges prevailing orthodoxies, and promotes the discovery of new solutions to societal problems. It provides individuals with the opportunity to engage in open dialogue, learn from each other's perspectives, and collectively shape the direction of our society.

7.1.3 The Connection Between Free Speech and Human Rights

Free speech is intricately linked to the broader framework of human rights. It enables individuals to exercise their right to freedom of thought, conscience, and expression. Free speech is essential for the functioning of a free society, as it allows citizens to voice their opinions, engage in political participation, and contribute to the public sphere.

Furthermore, free speech plays a critical role in exposing human rights abuses and advancing equality. It empowers marginalized communities to speak out against injustice, challenge systemic discrimination, and advocate for their rights.

Protecting and preserving free speech is, therefore, essential for upholding human rights principles and promoting a just and inclusive society.

7.2 The Threat of Censorship

7.2.1 The Rise of Online Platforms and Content Moderation

The advent of the internet and social media platforms has revolutionized communication and information sharing. However, it has also raised concerns about the power of these platforms to regulate speech and control the flow of information. Content moderation policies implemented by online platforms have the potential to impact the boundaries of free speech in the digital age.

While some level of moderation is necessary to address issues such as harassment, violent speech, and other illegal content, concerns arise when content moderation practices become subjective, inconsistent, or biased. The concentration of power in the hands of a few platform operators raises questions about the extent to which private entities should be responsible for regulating speech and the potential implications for free expression.

7.2.2 The Challenges of Political Correctness and Cancel Culture

Another threat to free speech arises from the phenomenon of political correctness and cancel culture. In recent years, there has been a growing trend of silencing individuals or ideas deemed offensive or contrary to prevailing social and political narratives. This stifling of dissenting voices through public shaming, online harassment, or professional consequences can have a chilling effect on free expression and discourage open dialogue.

The rise of cancel culture raises concerns about self-censorship, as individuals may fear expressing unpopular opinions or engaging in controversial discussions due to potential backlash. This erosion of free speech limits the diversity of ideas and impedes the discovery of truth through open debate and intellectual inquiry.

7.2.3 Global Challenges to Free Speech

The challenges to free speech are not limited to any specific region; they are global in nature. In various parts of the world, governments impose restrictions on speech, censor dissenting voices, and control the flow of information. Authoritarian regimes use censorship as a means to suppress opposition, consolidate power, and maintain social control.

Moreover, the emergence of digital authoritarianism and surveillance technologies poses new challenges to free speech. Governments exploit advanced technologies to monitor and censor online communications, infringing upon individuals' right to express themselves freely and access information without fear of reprisal.

7.3 Protecting Free Speech

7.3.1 Preserving Online Free Expression

To protect free speech in the digital age, it is essential to strike a balance between the need for content moderation and the preservation of online free expression. Online platforms should adopt transparent and consistent content moderation policies that prioritize the protection of lawful speech while addressing legitimate concerns related to harassment, incitement to violence, or illegal activities.

Efforts should also be made to promote competition and diversity among online platforms, reducing the risk of monopolistic control over speech regulation. Encouraging the development of alternative platforms that prioritize free expression can provide individuals with more choices and foster a healthier online ecosystem.

7.3.2 Fostering a Culture of Open Dialogue

To combat the challenges of political correctness and cancel culture, fostering a culture of open dialogue and respectful disagreement is crucial. Educational institutions, media organizations, and civil society should promote intellectual diversity, encourage free expression, and protect individuals' rights to hold and express diverse opinions.

Public figures, educators, and thought leaders have a responsibility to defend free speech and engage in constructive dialogue that challenges prevailing narratives without resorting to personal attacks or character assassination. Encouraging empathy, understanding, and active listening can create an environment where different perspectives can coexist, fostering robust and meaningful conversations.

7.3.3 International Efforts to Protect Free Speech

The protection of free speech requires international cooperation and advocacy. International organizations, such as the United Nations and non-governmental organizations, play a crucial role in promoting and defending free speech globally. They raise awareness about violations of free speech rights, provide support to individuals and groups facing censorship, and advocate for policies that safeguard free expression.

Additionally, digital rights activists and organizations work to combat internet censorship, support online privacy, and advocate for the protection of free speech in the digital realm. These efforts aim to ensure that individuals worldwide can exercise their right to free expression and access information without fear of repression.

7.4 A Comparison: King George vs. Free Expression

7.4.1 Suppression of Dissent and Freedom of Expression

During the colonial era, King George III's government sought to suppress dissent and control the flow of information. Restrictions on the press, censorship, and the stifling of political opposition limited free expression and impeded the colonists' ability to challenge unjust policies or voice their grievances.

The struggle for independence and the subsequent inclusion of free speech protections in the First Amendment reflected the recognition of the inherent value of free expression and the need to protect it as a fundamental right.

7.4.2 Defending Free Speech Today

To defend free speech today, we must remain vigilant against attempts to stifle dissenting voices, limit public discourse, or control the narrative. Upholding the principles of free speech requires an unwavering commitment to protecting individuals' rights to express their opinions, even when those opinions are unpopular or controversial.

By actively defending and exercising our right to free speech, engaging in open dialogue, and fostering a culture of respectful disagreement, we can ensure that free expression remains a cornerstone of our republic, allowing for the robust exchange of thoughts, knowledge, and perspectives.

Conclusion:

Free speech is a vital component of free societies, enabling open discourse, promoting intellectual diversity, and fostering societal progress. The rise of online platforms and the challenges posed by political correctness and cancel culture necessitate a proactive approach to protect and preserve free speech.

By establishing transparent content moderation policies, encouraging competition among online platforms, fostering a culture of open dialogue, and supporting international efforts to protect free speech, we can uphold the principles of free expression in the digital age and beyond. By defending free speech as a fundamental right and valuing the diversity of ideas, we can ensure that our society thrives on the free exchange of thoughts, knowledge, and perspectives.

Furthermore, it is crucial to recognize that the protection of free speech is an ongoing endeavor. As technology advances and new challenges emerge, we must adapt our strategies to safeguard free expression. Through continued advocacy, education, and a commitment to upholding the principles of free speech, we can create a future where diverse voices are heard, open dialogue flourishes and the republican ideals upon which our society is built are upheld.

References:

- Mill, John Stuart. On Liberty. 1859.
- Sunstein, Cass R. #Republic: Divided Democracy in the Age of Social Media. Princeton University Press, 2017.
- Volokh, Eugene. Freedom of Speech and Information Privacy: The Troubling Implications of a Right to Stop People from Speaking About You. Stanford Law Review, 2000.
- Fishkin, James S., and Laslett, Peter. Debating Deliberative Democracy. Wiley, 2003.
- West, Cornel, and Lott, Tommy. Free Speech: Ten Principles for a Connected World. Yale University Press, 2017.
- Office of the United Nations High Commissioner for Human Rights. International Covenant on Civil and Political Rights. 1966.

8

Preserving Privacy in the Digital Age

8.1 The Importance of Privacy

8.1.1 Privacy as a Fundamental Right

Privacy is a fundamental human right that underpins individual autonomy, personal dignity, and freedom. It encompasses the ability to control one's personal information, make choices about its disclosure, and maintain boundaries between the public and private spheres of life. The right to privacy is recognized and protected by numerous international declarations, conventions, and legal frameworks.

"The right to privacy is one of the most cherished liberties, for it is the foundation upon which other essential rights and freedoms rest." - Ron Wyden

Privacy is essential for the development of personal relationships, the formation of identities, and the exercise of freedom of thought, expression, and association. It enables individuals to express themselves authentically, without fear of judgment or surveillance, and fosters a sense of security and trust within society.

8.1.2 Privacy and the Digital Revolution

The digital revolution has transformed the way we live, work, and interact. While it has brought numerous benefits, it has also raised concerns about the erosion of privacy. The vast amount of personal information generated and collected in the digital realm, coupled with sophisticated data analytics and surveillance technologies, has created new challenges for privacy protection.

As individuals increasingly rely on digital platforms, social media, and online services, their personal data is often collected, analyzed, and shared without their full understanding or consent. The collection and aggregation of personal data by both public and private entities pose risks to privacy, autonomy, and individual control over personal information.

8.2 The Threats to Privacy

8.2.1 Surveillance and Mass Data Collection

One of the primary threats to privacy in the digital age is pervasive surveillance and mass data collection. Governments, intelligence agencies, and private entities engage in the collection and analysis of vast amounts of personal data, often without clear justification, oversight, or transparency. Surveillance technologies, such as facial recognition systems, biometric data collection, and bulk data interception, further amplify these concerns.

> "The balance between national security and individual privacy is a delicate one. We must ensure that government surveillance measures respect the privacy rights of individuals and are subject to robust oversight and accountability." - Patrick Leahy

Mass data collection and surveillance have the potential to undermine individual privacy, chill freedom of expression, and erode trust in digital services. The indiscriminate gathering and analysis of personal data can lead to profiling, discrimination, and the abuse of power. It is essential to strike a balance between legitimate security concerns and the protection of individual privacy rights.

8.2.2 Data Breaches and Cybersecurity

The proliferation of digital platforms and the vast amount of personal data stored electronically have also increased the risks of data breaches and cyberattacks. Malicious actors exploit vulnerabilities in information systems to gain unauthorized access to sensitive data, leading to identity theft, financial fraud, and the exposure of personal information.

Data breaches not only compromise individuals' privacy but also erode trust in online services and the digital economy as a whole. The protection of personal data and robust cybersecurity measures are crucial for maintaining privacy and ensuring the security of individuals' sensitive information.

8.3 Safeguarding Privacy in the Digital Age

8.3.1 Strong Legal Frameworks and Regulation

To protect privacy in the digital age, it is essential to establish strong legal frameworks and regulations that address the collection, storage, use, and sharing of personal data. Privacy laws should provide clear guidelines on how personal information can be collected, processed, and protected. They should also establish mechanisms for obtaining informed consent, notifying individuals of data breaches, and enabling individuals to exercise their rights over their personal information.

Regulatory bodies should have the authority and resources to enforce privacy laws effectively. Collaboration between governments, civil society organizations, and technology companies can lead to the development of robust privacy standards and best practices that align with evolving technological landscapes.

8.3.2 Privacy by Design and Data Minimization

Privacy should be incorporated into the design and development of digital technologies and services. Privacy by design principles emphasize embedding privacy features and safeguards into the architecture of systems, ensuring that privacy is considered from the outset rather than as an afterthought.

Data minimization practices should also be embraced, limiting the collection and retention of personal data to what is necessary for a specific purpose. Implementing privacy-enhancing technologies, such as encryption and anonymization, can further protect personal information and mitigate the risks of data breaches and unauthorized access.

8.3.3 Empowering Individuals and Enhancing Transparency

Individuals must have control over their personal information and be empowered to make informed choices about its use. Providing individuals with clear and understandable information about data collection practices, purposes, and potential risks enables them to make privacy-conscious decisions.

Transparency is crucial in building trust between individuals and organizations. Individuals should have access to their personal data held by organizations, the ability to correct inaccuracies, and the option to opt out of certain data collection practices. User-friendly privacy settings and tools that allow individuals to customize their privacy preferences can enhance control and empower individuals in the digital ecosystem.

8.4 A Comparison: King George vs. Privacy Rights

8.4.1 Invasion of Privacy and Unlawful Searches

During the colonial era, King George III's government authorized invasive searches, including unwarranted searches of homes and properties, to maintain control over the colonies. These actions violated the colonists' privacy and sparked outrage and resistance.

The fight for independence and the subsequent adoption of the Fourth Amendment to the United States Constitution reflected the recognition of the right to privacy and the need to protect individuals from unreasonable searches and seizures.

8.4.2 Defending Privacy Rights Today

To defend privacy rights today, we must be proactive in protecting personal data, ensuring transparency and accountability in data practices, and advocating for strong legal frameworks that safeguard privacy in the digital age. By demanding robust privacy protections, supporting organizations that promote privacy rights, and making privacy-conscious choices in our own digital lives, we can uphold privacy as a fundamental human right.

Conclusion:

Privacy is a fundamental human right that must be protected in the digital age. The advancements in technology and the proliferation of digital platforms should not come at the cost of sacrificing privacy. By establishing strong legal frameworks, promoting privacy by design, empowering individuals, and enhancing transparency, we can preserve privacy rights while harnessing the benefits of the digital revolution.

The fight for privacy in the digital age requires collective action, collaboration, and a commitment to upholding the principles of autonomy, dignity, and freedom. By championing privacy as a fundamental right, we ensure that individuals' personal information remains protected, their autonomy respected, and the foundations of a free society upheld.

References:

- Warren, Samuel D., and Brandeis, Louis D. "The Right to Privacy." Harvard Law Review, 1890.
- Solove, Daniel J. Understanding Privacy. Harvard University Press, 2008.
- Clarke, Roger, and Wigan, Marcus. "You Can't Handle the Truth! Public and Private in an Age of Ubiquitous Genomic Sequencing." Vanderbilt Journal of Entertainment and Technology Law, 2011.
- Nissenbaum, Helen. Privacy in Context: Technology, Policy, and the Integrity of Social Life. Stanford Law Books, 2009.
- Information Commissioner's Office. "Privacy by Design." Accessed July 11, 2023. https://ico.org.uk/for-organisations/guide-to-data-protection/guide-to-the-general-data-protection-regulation-gdpr/principles/privacy-by-design-and-default/.

9

Restoring Civic Engagement and Active Citizenship

9.1 The Importance of Civic Engagement

9.1.1 The Foundations of Freedom

Civic engagement is essential for the functioning of a healthy free society. It encompasses active participation in the political process, community involvement, and the exercise of rights and responsibilities as citizens. The framers of the Constitution understood the significance of civic engagement in safeguarding republican ideals and ensuring the government's accountability to the people.

"We must return to the principles and values that guided our Founding Fathers. The Constitution provides the blueprint for a limited government that respects individual liberties and ensures a system of checks and balances." - Mike Lee

A thriving society relies on an engaged and informed citizenry that actively participates in public affairs, holds elected officials accountable, and contributes to the betterment of society. Civic engagement strengthens the social fabric, promotes inclusivity, and empowers individuals to shape the direction of their communities and the nation as a whole.

9.1.2 The Benefits of Active Citizenship

Active citizenship brings numerous benefits to both individuals and society. By actively engaging in civic life, individuals become more knowledgeable about political issues, gain a deeper understanding of public policies, and develop critical thinking and problem-solving skills. Active citizens are more likely to vote, volunteer, and participate in community organizations, fostering social cohesion and collective action.

Moreover, active citizenship strengthens the legitimacy of democratic institutions by ensuring that policies and decisions reflect the will and interests of the people. When citizens are engaged and actively involved, they can influence the political agenda, advocate for their concerns, and contribute to the democratic and representative processes.

9.2 The Decline of Civic Engagement

9.2.1 Political Apathy and Disillusionment

In recent years, there has been a decline in civic engagement and a growing sense of political apathy and disillusionment among the public. Many citizens feel disconnected from the political process, viewing it as distant, unresponsive, and dominated by special interests. This disengagement can lead to a diminished sense of civic responsibility and a weakened republic.

Factors contributing to the decline in civic engagement include increasing polarization, the influence of money in politics, and a perceived lack of transparency and accountability in government. The rise of social media and digital technologies, while offering new avenues for participation, has also brought challenges such as the spread of misinformation and the fragmentation of public discourse.

9.2.2 Barriers to Participation

Various barriers hinder active citizenship and civic engagement. Socioeconomic disparities, unequal access to education and information, and a lack of representation can limit individuals' ability to participate fully in the political process. Systemic inequalities, voter suppression, and restrictive policies can disproportionately affect marginalized communities, further eroding trust and engagement.

Additionally, a lack of civics education and media literacy contributes to a lack of understanding of processes and institutions. When citizens are unaware of their rights, the importance of their voice, and how to effectively engage, it becomes challenging to cultivate an active and informed citizenry.

9.3 Restoring Civic Engagement

9.3.1 Strengthening Civic Education

Civic education plays a crucial role in fostering active citizenship and promoting civic engagement. By prioritizing comprehensive and inclusive civics education in schools, we can equip young people with the knowledge, skills, and values necessary to participate in political processes, critically analyze information, and engage in constructive dialogue.

Civic education should focus on teaching the principles and values that underpin our republic, the rights and responsibilities of citizenship, the importance of civic discourse, and the tools for effective civic action. It should encourage active learning experiences, such as debates, simulations, and community projects, to provide practical opportunities for students to engage in civic life.

9.3.2 Encouraging Voter Participation

Voter participation is a critical component of civic engagement and representative decision-making. Efforts should be made to remove barriers to voting, enhance access to voter registration, and promote voter education. Expanding early voting options, ensuring language accessibility, and implementing automatic voter registration can increase voter turnout and enhance the inclusivity of the electoral process.

Furthermore, campaigns and initiatives should aim to educate citizens about the importance of their vote and the impact of their participation. Encouraging voter registration drives, fostering dialogue on civic issues, and promoting community-based initiatives can raise awareness and inspire citizens to exercise their right to vote.

9.3.3 Facilitating Community Engagement

Community engagement is vital for building social capital, fostering trust, and addressing local challenges. Encouraging citizens to actively participate in community organizations, neighborhood associations, and volunteer activities can strengthen social cohesion and empower individuals to make a positive impact.

Government agencies and community leaders should facilitate opportunities for citizen participation in decision-making processes, policy formulation, and community planning. Emphasizing transparency, accountability, and responsiveness can help rebuild trust in institutions and inspire citizens to engage in civic life.

9.4 A Comparison: King George vs. Active Citizenship

9.4.1 Limited Participation and Lack of Representation

Under King George's rule, the American colonists experienced limited participation in decision-making processes and lacked representation in government. The colonists' fight for independence and the subsequent establishment of a democratic representative system reflected their desire for increased civic engagement, political participation, and a government that is accountable to the people.

9.4.2 Upholding Active Citizenship Today

To uphold active citizenship today, we must be proactive in promoting civic education, breaking down barriers to participation, and fostering inclusive and accessible processes. By providing comprehensive civics education, ensuring equal access to voting, and creating opportunities for meaningful community engagement, we can foster an environment where active citizenship thrives.

Political leaders, educators, and community organizations have a responsibility to promote active citizenship by modeling republican values, encouraging civic participation, and amplifying the voices of citizens. By creating platforms for dialogue, embracing diversity, and fostering a culture of civic responsibility, we can restore faith in the political process and empower citizens to actively contribute to the well-being of their communities and society as a whole.

Conclusion:

Restoring civic engagement is crucial for the health and vibrancy of freedom. By prioritizing civic education, promoting voter participation, facilitating community engagement, and upholding the principles of active citizenship, we can revitalize civic life, ensure inclusive decision-making, and empower individuals to actively contribute to the betterment of their communities and society.

The fight to restore civic engagement requires a collective effort, recognizing that active citizenship is the foundation of a strong and thriving republic. By embracing the rights and responsibilities of citizenship, we can create a society where the voices of all citizens are heard, respected, and valued, fostering a more just, equitable, and participatory future.

References:

- Hess, Diana E., and McAvoy, Paula. The Political Classroom: Evidence and Ethics in Democratic Education. Routledge, 2015.
- Kahne, Joseph, and Westheimer, Joel. "Teaching Democracy: What Schools Need to Do." Phi Delta Kappan, 2003.
- Levine, Peter. "Building a Civic Infrastructure for a Digital Age." Civic Media: Technology, Design, Practice, MIT Press, 2016.
- Leighley, Jan E., and Nagler, Jonathan. Who Votes Now? Demographics, Issues, Inequality, and Turnout in the United States. Princeton University Press, 2014.
- Lijphart, Arend. Electoral Systems and Party Systems: A Study of Twenty-Seven Democracies, 1945-1990. Oxford University Press, 1994.
- Plutzer, Eric. "Becoming a Habitual Voter: Inertia, Resources, and Growth in Young Adulthood." American Political Science Review, 2002.
- Putnam, Robert D. Bowling Alone: The Collapse and Revival of American Community. Simon & Schuster, 2000.
- Warren, Mark R. "What Can Democratic Participation Mean Today?" Political Theory, 2017.
- Emerson, Karen. "The Oxford Handbook of Political Networks." Oxford University Press, 2017.
- Wood, Gordon S. The Radicalism of the American Revolution. Vintage, 1993.
- Young, Alfred F. The Shoemaker and the Tea Party: Memory and the American Revolution. Beacon Press, 1999.
- Middlekauff, Robert. The Glorious Cause: The American

Revolution, 1763-1789. Oxford University Press, 2005.

- Barber, Benjamin R. Strong Democracy: Participatory Politics for a New Age. University of California Press, 2004.
- Putnam, Robert D., et al. "Tuning In, Tuning Out: The Strange Disappearance of Social Capital in America." PS: Political Science & Politics, 2000.
- Skocpol, Theda. Diminished Democracy: From Membership to Management in American Civic Life. University of Oklahoma Press, 2003.

10

Preserving the Power of the People: The Bill of Rights and the Jury System

In this chapter, we delve into the heart of the Bill of Rights, a testament to the Founding Fathers' unwavering commitment to safeguarding individual liberties and ensuring a just society. Central to this constitutional safeguard is the cherished institution of the jury system, a time-honored pillar of western governance. We explore the Founders' foresight in enshrining the right to trial by jury in the Fifth, Sixth, and Seventh Amendments, affirming the essential role of citizen participation in the administration of justice. As we journey through the historical significance of these rights, we uncover the origins of the jury's power, rooted in the concept of natural law and the profound belief in the wisdom of the people. This chapter pays homage to the jury's duty as fact-finder and protector of rights, as well as its role in safeguarding the people's power to nullify unjust laws.

10.1 The Role of the Jury in the Bill of Rights

The Founding Fathers recognized the vital role of the jury system in safeguarding individual liberties and ensuring the administration of justice. Consequently, they enshrined the right to a trial by jury in the Fifth, Sixth, and Seventh Amendments of the Bill of Rights. These amendments are a testament to the Founders' commitment to protecting citizens from arbitrary government actions and ensuring fair and impartial trials.

The Fifth Amendment, with its due process clause, guarantees that no person shall be deprived of life, liberty, or property without due process of law. This essential safeguard ensures that individuals facing criminal charges or potential government actions are entitled to a fair and just trial. It also serves as a barrier against arbitrary arrests or detentions, affirming that no one shall be deprived of their fundamental rights without proper legal proceedings.

> "No person shall be... deprived of life, liberty, or property, without due process of law..." - The Fifth Amendment of the United States Constitution

The Sixth Amendment solidifies the right to a fair trial by an impartial jury. It establishes the right to a speedy and public trial, granting individuals the opportunity to face their accusers and present evidence in their defense. By ensuring the trial's public nature, the Sixth Amendment reinforces transparency and accountability in the judicial process.

> "In all criminal prosecutions, the accused shall enjoy the right to a speedy and public trial, by an impartial jury of the State and district wherein the crime shall have been committed…" - The Sixth Amendment of the United States Constitution

The Seventh Amendment extends the jury trial right to civil cases where the value in controversy exceeds twenty dollars. This provision ensures that parties involved in civil disputes have their cases heard and decided by a jury of their peers, safeguarding their rights and protecting against potential abuses of power by the government or other entities.

> "In suits at common law, where the value in controversy shall exceed twenty dollars, the right of trial by jury shall be preserved…" - The Seventh Amendment of the United States Constitution

10.2 Grievances Against the King and the Judiciary

The grievances enumerated in the Declaration of Independence reflect the colonists' frustration with the king's abuse of power, particularly in the realm of the judiciary. King George III obstructed the administration of justice by refusing his assent to laws establishing judicial powers, undermining the establishment of a fair and independent judiciary in the American colonies.

> "He has obstructed the administration of justice by refusing his assent to laws for establishing judiciary powers." - Excerpt from the Declaration of Independence

The colonists' experience with King George III emphasized the importance of creating a judicial system that would protect the people's rights and liberties. By limiting the government's arbitrary powers and providing a framework for impartial adjudication, the Founders aimed to ensure that justice would prevail and that individuals would be protected from the whims of the executive.

10.3 The Power of Jury Nullification

The notion of jury nullification harks back to the historical concept of jury independence, which allows jurors to deliver a verdict based on their conscience and their understanding of justice. Noah Webster's 1828 dictionary defines a jury as a group of individuals impaneled and sworn to inquire into and try any matter of fact, and to declare the truth on the evidence given in the case. This definition underscores the jury's critical role as a fact-finder, whose purpose is to reach a verdict based on the evidence presented in the trial.

> "A jury consists usually of twelve men, who try the merits of a cause between the parties, and are jurors of the facts." - Noah Webster, "An American Dictionary of the English Language" (1828)

Jury nullification, a concept deeply ingrained in the Anglo-American legal tradition, grants jurors the authority to acquit a defendant despite evidence of guilt if they believe the law itself is unjust or has been applied unfairly. This power empowers ordinary citizens to act as a final check against oppressive legislation or government actions, ensuring that the spirit of justice prevails even in cases where the strict letter of the law may dictate otherwise.

> "It is not only [the juror's] right, but his duty... to find the verdict according to his own best understanding, judgment, and conscience, though in direct opposition to the direction of the court." - John Adams

10.4 Efforts to Eliminate Jury Trials: Challenges to the People's Power

While the Founders intended the jury system to serve as a safeguard against government overreach, there have been instances where efforts have been made to eliminate jury trials in some cases in certain states. Critics of the jury system argue that it can be inefficient and time-consuming, leading some jurisdictions to explore alternative methods of resolving legal disputes. One such approach has been the implementation of mandatory arbitration or mediation programs in civil cases, which aim to streamline the resolution process without resorting to a traditional jury trial.

However, these efforts have raised concerns about potential infringements on the people's power to participate in the administration of justice. By replacing jury trials with administrative procedures or non-judicial forums, there is a risk of diminishing the public's voice in legal proceedings and diluting the citizenry's role in shaping the outcome of cases.

Additionally, in some criminal cases, proposals to limit jury trials for certain offenses or circumstances have been met with opposition. Advocates of preserving the right to trial by jury assert that any attempt to restrict this constitutional right undermines the principles of fairness and accountability enshrined in the Bill of Rights.

> "Trial by jury in criminal cases is as essential to secure the liberty of the people as any one of the pre-existent rights of nature." - James Madison

Conclusion:

The Founding Fathers recognized the pivotal role of the jury system in preserving individual liberties and ensuring the rule of law. By enshrining the right to trial by jury in the Bill of Rights and empowering jurors with the authority to nullify unjust laws, the Founders ensured that the power of the people would forever serve as a check on the government's potential abuses. The jury's duty to uphold justice and protect individual rights remains an enduring testament to the wisdom and foresight of the Framers in creating a democratic republic that places ultimate sovereignty in the hands of the people.

References:

- The Constitution of the United States of America, Bill of Rights, Amendments V, VI, and VII.
- The Declaration of Independence.
- Webster, Noah. "An American Dictionary of the English Language." 1828.

11

Conclusion

Reclaiming the Spirit of Liberty

As we come to the end of our exploration in "A More Tyrannical King: How the Federal Government Has Become More Oppressive Than King George," we find ourselves at a critical juncture in the history of our nation. We have examined the alarming expansion of the federal government, the encroachments on individual liberties, and the erosion of the principles that once guided our republic. But this journey has not been one of despair; rather, it has been a call to action, a reminder of the power we hold as citizens to shape the destiny of our nation.

Throughout the preceding chapters, we have presented a compelling case for returning to constitutional principles as the only way to save our republic. We have examined the wisdom of our Founding Fathers, their intent to create a limited government, and their commitment to protecting the rights and freedoms of the people. We have seen how the federal government, over time, has deviated from these principles, assuming powers never intended by the Constitution.

But the story does not end here. We have the power to reclaim the spirit of liberty that once animated our nation. It starts with recognizing the importance of active citizenship, of each individual playing a role in the political process. We must embrace the responsibilities and duties of being informed, engaged citizens who hold our elected officials accountable and actively participate in shaping the decisions that impact our lives.

Restoring our republic requires a collective effort. It necessitates fostering an environment that values civil discourse, respects differing opinions, and upholds the principles of free speech and open dialogue. We must reject the politics of division and embrace the principles that unite us as a nation. By transcending partisan lines and finding common ground, we can work together to rebuild a government that truly serves the people.

Education is also a crucial element in this journey. We must prioritize civic education in our schools, ensuring that future generations understand the principles upon which our nation was built. By equipping young minds with a comprehensive understanding of our Constitution, the rights it protects, and the responsibilities it bestows upon us, we can cultivate a new generation of active, informed, and engaged citizens.

Furthermore, we must demand transparency and accountability from our government. We must advocate for a reduction in the power of the administrative state, a restoration of states' rights, and a renewed commitment to protecting individual liberties. It is through these measures that we can safeguard the checks and balances that were designed to prevent the concentration of power in the hands of a few.

The path ahead may be challenging, but we are not alone. History has shown us that the flame of liberty can be rekindled even in the darkest times. It is our duty to carry that torch forward, to ensure that the principles enshrined in our Constitution are not mere words on parchment but living, breathing guides for our governance.

As we conclude this book, we invite you, our readers, to reflect upon the ideas presented, to engage in conversations that transcend political lines, and to join the movement to restore our republic. We encourage you to remain vigilant, to question authority, and to hold steadfastly to the values of freedom, liberty, and limited government.

Together, let us reclaim the spirit of liberty that fueled the American Revolution, guided our Founding Fathers, and inspired generations of patriots. Let us work tirelessly to build a government that respects the rights of the people, cherishes our republican ideals, and secures a prosperous future for all.

Thank you for accompanying us on this journey, and may the principles of liberty and constitutional originalism guide our path towards a brighter, freer, and more prosperous America.

In the words of Thomas Jefferson, "We hold these truths to be self-evident, that all men are created equal, that they are endowed by their Creator with certain unalienable Rights, that among these are Life, Liberty and the pursuit of Happiness." It is our duty to preserve and protect these unalienable rights for ourselves and future generations.

Together, let us ensure that the flame of freedom burns bright, illuminating the path towards a more just and prosperous future.

God bless America.

Afterword

Reclaiming Our Republic - Restoring Power to the People

As we reach the conclusion of "A More Tyrannical King: How the Federal Government Has Become More Oppressive Than King George," we find ourselves standing at a crucial crossroad in the history of our nation. The journey through the chapters of this book has shed light on the challenges we face, but it is in this afterward that we look forward with hope and determination. Now is the time to explore tangible ways in which we can regain control of our government and restore power to the people.

1. Active Citizenship: The foundation of reclaiming our republic lies in the active participation of citizens. We must recognize our role as informed and engaged individuals in shaping the course of our nation. It begins with educating ourselves on the principles of our Constitution, understanding our rights and responsibilities, and staying informed about political issues.

2. Grassroots Movements: History has shown us that grass-

roots movements have the power to effect change. By organizing at the local level, building networks of like-minded individuals, and advocating for our values, we can create a groundswell of support for constitutional principles and limited government. Engaging with community organizations, attending town hall meetings, and participating in peaceful protests can amplify our collective voice.

3. Voting with Purpose: The ballot box remains one of the most potent tools for expressing our will as citizens. By voting with purpose and informed decision-making, we can hold elected officials accountable and support candidates who align with our vision of limited government and individual liberties. It is essential to research candidates, their positions, and their records to ensure they uphold the principles we hold dear.

4. Engaging in Public Discourse: The exchange of ideas and civil discourse are crucial components of a healthy society. We must actively engage in public discourse, not only by sharing our viewpoints but also by actively listening to others. By fostering respectful dialogue and seeking common ground, we can bridge divides and find solutions that uphold our constitutional ideals.

5. Supporting Constitutional Advocacy Groups: There are numerous organizations dedicated to protecting and promoting constitutional principles. Supporting these groups through donations, volunteering, or active participation can amplify our collective efforts. By joining forces with like-minded individuals, we can pool our resources and make a greater impact in defending our liberties.

6. Encouraging Constitutional Education: We must prioritize constitutional education at all levels of our society. By advocating for comprehensive civics education in schools, promoting constitutional literacy programs, and supporting initiatives that enhance understanding of our founding documents, we can ensure that future generations are equipped with the knowledge and appreciation of our constitutional heritage.

7. Running for Office: To effect meaningful change, we must actively participate in the political process. Consider running for local, state, or federal office to bring a fresh perspective and a commitment to constitutional principles. By stepping up to serve, we can contribute to the governance of our nation and champion the values we hold dear.

8. Embracing Technological Tools: In the digital age, technology can be harnessed to empower citizens and increase transparency in government. Embrace the use of digital platforms and social media to disseminate information, mobilize support, and hold elected officials accountable. By leveraging these tools responsibly, we can foster a more connected and engaged citizenry.

9. Strengthening State and Local Governance: Reinvigorating federalism and supporting robust state and local governments can help check the concentration of power at the federal level. By engaging with local political processes, advocating for stronger state rights, and supporting candidates committed to devolving power to local communities, we can create a system that is more responsive to the needs and values of the people.

The road to reclaiming our republic may be challenging, but it is not insurmountable. It requires collective action, unwavering commitment, and an enduring belief in the power of the people. As we conclude this book, let us embrace the responsibility that comes with the privilege of citizenship. Let us engage in constructive dialogue, inspire others to join us on this journey, and work tirelessly to ensure that our government remains true to its founding principles.

Together, we can restore power to the people, reignite the flame of liberty, and secure a future where the principles of our Constitution guide our nation towards greatness. The time to reclaim our republic is now.

Definitions

These definitions from Webster's 1828 Dictionary offer valuable insights into the meanings of these terms as understood during the time of the Founding Fathers. In order to understand the original intent, we must understand the words they used and the meanings of those words at the time they were written.

1. Common Law: "The customary law, or that which is established by long usage, in distinction from the written or statute law. The common law of England is unwritten or lex non scripta, and depends for its authority on the universal reception of immemorial usage. The common law is founded on reason, and is the perfection of reason."
2. Despotism: "Absolute power; authority unlimited and uncontrolled by men, constitution or laws, and depending alone on the will of the prince; as the *despotism* of a Turkish sultan."
3. Emolument: "The profit arising from office or employment; that which is received as a compensation for services, or which is annexed to the possession of office, as salary, fees, or perquisites."
4. Inestimable: "Not capable of being estimated or computed; too valuable or excellent to be measured or appreciated;

invaluable; as, inestimable benefits or advantages."

5. Jury: "A number of men, usually twelve, selected according to law, impaneled and sworn to inquire into and try any matter of fact, and to declare the truth on the evidence given in the case. This is the office of jurors in civil and criminal trials."

6. Militia: "In the widest sense, the whole military force of a nation, including both those engaged in military service as a business and those competent and available for such service; specifically, the body of citizens enrolled for military instruction and discipline, but not subject to active duty except in emergencies, as distinguished from regular troops or a standing army."

7. Misdemeanors: "In law, an offense of a less atrocious nature than a crime. Crimes and misdemeanors are mere synonymous terms; but in common usage, the word crime is made to denote offenses of a deeper and more atrocious dye, while small faults and omissions of less consequence are comprised under the gentler name of misdemeanors."

8. Natural Law: "A rule of conduct arising out of the natural relations of human beings established by the Creator, and existing prior to any positive precept. Thus it is a natural law that one man should not injure another, and murder and fraud would be crimes, independent of any prohibition from a supreme power."

9. Providence: "The care and superintendence which God exercises over his creatures. He that acknowledges a creation and denies a providence involves himself in a palpable contradiction; for the same power which caused a thing to exist is necessary to continue its existence."

10. Regulated: "Adjusted by rule, method, or forms; put in

good order; subjected to rules or restrictions. A house is regulated when the furniture is disposed in the manner intended by the owner; commerce is regulated by law; our appetites and passions should be regulated by reason; our conduct should be regulated by the precepts of the gospel."

11. Remiss: "Not energetic or exact in duty or business; not careful or prompt in performing duty; negligent; careless; tardy."

12. Republican: "Pertaining to a republic; consisting of a commonwealth; as a *republican* constitution or government."

13. Tyranny: "Arbitrary or despotic exercise of power; the exercise of power over subjects and others with a rigor not authorized by law or justice, or not requisite for the purposes of government."

14. Unalienable: "Not to be separated, given away or taken away; that cannot be transferred to another. All men have certain natural rights which are unalienable."

15. Usurpation: "The act of seizing or occupying and enjoying the property of another, without right; as the *usurpation* of a throne; the *usurpation* of the supreme power."

Declaration of Independence

No comparison of tyranny or oppression in the United States would be complete without the Declaration of Independence. We should all pay close attention to the twenty-seven grievances against King George as we consider the grievances we have against our current government.

IN CONGRESS, July 4, 1776.

The unanimous Declaration of the thirteen united States of America,

When in the Course of human events, it becomes necessary for one people to dissolve the political bands which have connected them with another, and to assume among the powers of the earth, the separate and equal station to which the Laws of Nature and of Nature's God entitle them, a decent respect to the opinions of mankind requires that they should declare the causes which impel them to the separation.

We hold these truths to be self-evident, that all men are created equal, that they are endowed by their Creator with certain unalienable Rights, that among these are Life, Liberty and the pursuit of Happiness.–That to secure these rights, Governments are instituted among Men, deriving their just powers from the consent of the governed, –That whenever any Form of Government becomes destructive of these ends, it is the Right of the People to alter or to abolish it, and to institute new Government, laying its foundation on such principles and organizing its powers in such form, as to them shall seem most likely to effect their Safety and Happiness. Prudence, indeed, will dictate that Governments long established should not be changed for light and transient causes; and accordingly all experience hath shewn, that mankind are more disposed to suffer, while evils are sufferable, than to right themselves by abolishing the forms to which they are accustomed. But when a long train of abuses and usurpations, pursuing invariably the same Object evinces a design to reduce them under absolute Despotism, it is their right, it is their duty, to throw off such Government, and to provide new Guards for their future security.–Such has been the patient sufferance of these Colonies; and such is now the necessity which constrains them to alter their former Systems of Government. The history of the present King of Great Britain is a history of repeated injuries and usurpations, all having in direct object the establishment of an absolute Tyranny over these States. To prove this, let Facts be submitted to a candid world.

He has refused his Assent to Laws, the most wholesome and necessary for the public good.

He has forbidden his Governors to pass Laws of immediate and pressing importance, unless suspended in their operation till his Assent should be obtained; and when so suspended, he has utterly neglected to attend to them.

He has refused to pass other Laws for the accommodation of large districts of people, unless those people would relinquish the right of Representation in the Legislature, a right inestimable to them and formidable to tyrants only.

He has called together legislative bodies at places unusual, uncomfortable, and distant from the depository of their public Records, for the sole purpose of fatiguing them into compliance with his measures.

He has dissolved Representative Houses repeatedly, for opposing with manly firmness his invasions on the rights of the people.

He has refused for a long time, after such dissolutions, to cause others to be elected; whereby the Legislative powers, incapable of Annihilation, have returned to the People at large for their exercise; the State remaining in the mean time exposed to all the dangers of invasion from without, and convulsions within.

He has endeavoured to prevent the population of these States; for that purpose obstructing the Laws for Naturalization of Foreigners; refusing to pass others to encourage their migrations hither, and raising the conditions of new Appropriations of Lands.

He has obstructed the Administration of Justice, by refusing his Assent to Laws for establishing Judiciary powers.

He has made Judges dependent on his Will alone, for the tenure of their offices, and the amount and payment of their salaries.

He has erected a multitude of New Offices, and sent hither swarms of Officers to harrass our people, and eat out their substance.

He has kept among us, in times of peace, Standing Armies without the Consent of our legislatures.

He has affected to render the Military independent of and superior to the Civil power.He has combined with others to subject us to a jurisdiction foreign to our constitution, and unacknowledged by our laws; giving his Assent to their Acts of pretended Legislation:

For Quartering large bodies of armed troops among us:

For protecting them, by a mock Trial, from punishment for any Murders which they should commit on the Inhabitants of these States:

For cutting off our Trade with all parts of the world:

For imposing Taxes on us without our Consent:

For depriving us in many cases, of the benefits of Trial by Jury:

For transporting us beyond Seas to be tried for pretended offences

For abolishing the free System of English Laws in a neighbouring Province, establishing therein an Arbitrary government, and enlarging its Boundaries so as to render it at once an example and fit instrument for introducing the same absolute rule into these Colonies:

For taking away our Charters, abolishing our most valuable Laws, and altering fundamentally the Forms of our Governments:

For suspending our own Legislatures, and declaring themselves invested with power to legislate for us in all cases whatsoever.

He has abdicated Government here, by declaring us out of his Protection and waging War against us.

He has plundered our seas, ravaged our Coasts, burnt our towns, and destroyed the lives of our people.

He is at this time transporting large Armies of foreign Mercenaries to compleat the works of death, desolation and tyranny, already begun with circumstances of Cruelty & perfidy scarcely paralleled in the most barbarous ages, and totally unworthy the Head of a civilized nation.

He has constrained our fellow Citizens taken Captive on the high Seas to bear Arms against their Country, to become the executioners of their friends and Brethren, or to fall themselves by their Hands.

He has excited domestic insurrections amongst us, and has endeavoured to bring on the inhabitants of our frontiers, the merciless Indian Savages, whose known rule of warfare, is an undistinguished destruction of all ages, sexes and conditions.

In every stage of these Oppressions We have Petitioned for Redress in the most humble terms: Our repeated Petitions have been answered only by repeated injury. A Prince whose character is thus marked by every act which may define a Tyrant, is unfit to be the ruler of a free people.

Nor have We been wanting in attentions to our Brittish brethren. We have warned them from time to time of attempts by their legislature to extend an unwarrantable jurisdiction over us. We have reminded them of the circumstances of our emigration and settlement here. We have appealed to their native justice and magnanimity, and we have conjured them by the ties of our common kindred to disavow these usurpations, which, would inevitably interrupt our connections and correspondence. They too have been deaf to the voice of justice and of consanguinity. We must, therefore, acquiesce in the necessity, which denounces our Separation, and hold them, as we hold the rest of mankind, Enemies in War, in Peace Friends.

We, therefore, the Representatives of the united States of America, in General Congress, Assembled, appealing to the Supreme Judge of the world for the rectitude of our intentions, do, in the Name, and by Authority of the good People of these Colonies, solemnly publish and declare, That these United Colonies are, and of Right ought to be Free and Independent States; that they are Absolved from all Allegiance to the British Crown, and that all political connection between them and the State of Great Britain, is and ought to be totally dissolved; and that as Free and Independent States, they have full Power to levy War, conclude Peace, contract Alliances, establish Commerce, and to do all other Acts and Things which Independent States may of right do. And for the support of this Declaration, with a firm reliance on the protection of divine Providence, we mutually pledge to each other our Lives, our Fortunes and our sacred Honor.

About the Author

Peter Serefine, a proud U.S. Navy veteran and current U.S. Mail carrier, possesses a high school education and holds the office of Pennsylvania State Constable. A steadfast member of the diminishing middle class, he sought to make a difference amid the political turbulence of 2016. His initial work, "Progress, Really?", was authored with the intention of inspiring individuals to scrutinize the trajectory of social and political advancements. Peter expanded his impact by hosting the Liberty Lighthouse on Mojo 5-0 Radio, earning the affectionate title of possessing the best beard in radio from his fellow network hosts. With a commitment to civic education, he established the online Liberty Lighthouse Classroom to impart the principles of constitutional governance.

Despite his busy schedule of working full-time, writing op-ed articles, and now publishing three books, Peter continues to host a two-hour live radio show each week. Residing in a charming Victorian town in Pennsylvania, he shares his life with his beloved and beautiful partner Staisha Hancock, whose infinite patience gracefully accommodates Peter's fervent political discussions.

You can connect with me on:
- https://www.liberty-lighthouse.com
- https://twitter.com/PSerefine
- https://facebook.com/PSerefine

Also by Peter Serefine

Progress, Really?

★★★★★ This is a quick read about one perspective on the past, current, and future state of American culture, government, and social standing. The author points out many areas of our country that are straying from its fundamental basis and how continual complacency and acceptance of minority opinions for the sake of appeasing the entitled is quickly leading us toward socialism and an overall destruction of the founding fathers vision.

★★★★★ What the author chose as topics, happen to be some of the hottest topics in the U.S. as of 2019. Peter makes the reader think on his/her own, but provides different angles of thinking by giving plenty of references. The personification of progress is a clever way of persuading the reader to evaluate the path of American society.

So Simple Even A Politician Can Understand

☆☆☆☆☆ A great look at easy answers to fix our government and start a conversation between both sides. Think of this as an insightful beginner's guide to repair and simplify the machine that's out of control.

☆☆☆☆☆ The book like the title says is simple ideas we can push for meaningful change. Simple ideas to drive the cause of liberty.

☆☆☆☆☆ Great book, an easy read!! It's everything a lot of us are thinking… but can't quite put into words.

www.ingramcontent.com/pod-product-compliance
Lightning Source LLC
Chambersburg PA
CBHW070534160726
48003CB00004B/1782